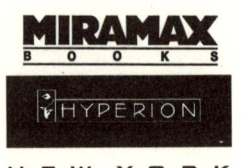

COPYRIGHT © 1994 MARTIN LAWRENCE

Photographs Copyright © 1994, Home Box Office, a Division of Time Warner Entertainment Company, L.P.

All rights reserved. No part of this book may be used or reproduced in any manner whatsoever without the written permission of the Publisher. Printed in the United States of America. For information address Hyperion, 114 Fifth Avenue, New York, New York 10011.

ISBN 0-7868-8083-X

FIRST EDITION
10 9 8 7 6 5 4 3 2 1

ONE

Racism fucks with me, man. It bothers me. America is the best country in the world, but I'm not getting no call during a war. They call me, I'm like this. I'm sorry. I can't motherfuckin' go. Already been in the war, motherfucker. My lady gonna say, "What you doing?" "Bitch, do what I do before they draft your ass." And I know there's some people out there—white people—going, "Oh, my God, is he on this whole racial thing?" But ask yourself does racism still exist? You motherfuckin' right it still exists. The Rodney King ass whipping was a prime example of that shit. And they didn't just whip Rodney's ass, they whizzazzazzazz . . . Rodney's ass. And Rodney kept getting up. I ain't understand that. Shit. I'd have been just like a little bitch chilling.

2

With a ass whoopin'. But see, Rodney kept getting up because, see, that's how black people are. We don't stay down for nobody. That's right. Rodney had that Kunta Kinte spirit in him and shit. You know. Remember fuckin' Kunta Kinte was running his ass off. Kunta said, "I got to be free." They cut off his foot, Kunta was like this . . . . They cut off both his feet, he just . . . "I's no longer gonna be with you." Racism is a motherfucker, man. That night, that whole Rodney King thing went on and we had a riot. Remember that shit? I know you remember that. White people even remember that, don't you? We wasn't bullshitting that night of the riots, was we? Was not playing that night. But that was the nicest white people had ever been, wasn't it? You could get over in traffic that night, couldn't you? "Excuse me, white man, can I get over?" "Sure, come on. Just come on. Fuckin' go ahead, buddy." They knew we was mad that night, too.

So they try to call what they call black heroes to calm us down. That's got me. Call Magic Johnson. "Come on, ya'll, this is Magic Johnson. Let's stop all the violence. Get back to showtime." Come on. Black people, man, you can't tell us shit.

We like, "Hey, Magic, we love you, you know,

YOU SO CRAZY

3

take your medication and sit your ass down." No. I say this is what we said that night, that's all. We didn't have nothing against Magic. We love Magic. I love Magic. But we was just mad that night. They even called Jesse Jackson. Trying, you know, Jesse Jackson show up every goddamn where. Jesse show up a high school fight. "Keep hope alive! Keep hope alive!" Keep your ass alive, Jesse. And sit the fuck down. Whose side you on? And then—then that night, man, I was watching television, they had the nerve to air *Driving Miss Daisy*. Showing you how shit used to be. Morgan Freeman talking that shit. "Oh, come on now, Miss Daisy. I's trying to drive you to the store." Shit. I wish I'da starred in that motherfucker. Dialogue would have been a little different. "Bitch, shut the fuck up. I'm trying to drive your stinking ass to the store. Suck my dick, Miss Daisy, you stank. Just get your ass up outta the car. Get the fuck up out of the car, bitch. Get your ass on out the car. And you better have my check." We weren't playing that night, ya'll. And the media was getting jokes in on us and shit. Wasn't it? Media think they slick.

White media have some jokes for you. "Oh, my God! Oh, my God! They just looted another super-

4

market. I can guarantee if you come down here all the chicken is gone. All the watermelon and malt liquor is gone." That's all they showed that night ... was black people coming out the store with shit. Black people. Black people coming out the store with shit. They even showed me one time coming out with some shit. You know, 'cause I had to be down with my people. But they didn't say shit about the Mexicans. Nothing. And tell the truth. Come on, now. The Mexicans got them some shit. I love the Mexicans—la vista and Chavez to you. But you got you some shit. And the Mexicans didn't even know what the cause was about. They just saw a opportunity to get some free shit. I had Mexicans roll up on me crying, "Yo, my man. This is fucked up. This should never fuckin' happen. The way they beat Rodney Dangerfield was wrong. He don't get no respect." It was crazy. We got to get over this racial hump. We have to. It's very important. What fucks me up, though, I just wish white people tell us what bothers them about us. Like, white people, I could tell you what bothers me about you.

You motherfuckers too chipper. You know this is your country. "Hello, darkie." "Move, darkie." They know this is America, man. I just wish white people

would admit to it. Like, white people, admit you hate like when you're in a movie theater and you see black people walk in a movie theater. Yeah, you want to get the black dollars, but you want us to see that shit in our own neighborhood. When they see black people walk in the theater they go, "Oh, fuck! Honey, look out. Look fuckin' out. The one in the X hat. Look at him. The one in the fuckin' X hat. Watch they come sit right behind us." 'Cause see white people know when black people walk in a movie theater, they ain't gonna see the movie. 'Cause we gonna talk all the way through that motherfucker. And you know that's just black people, we emotional like that. And we don't holler corny shit out in the movie. White people holler corny shit out in the movie: "Look out." "Watch out." "I hope he doesn't get hurt." "Someone hold your horses." Black people don't do that shit. "Watch out, bitch! The motherfucker got the knife." "Bitch, watch it! Oh, you dumb-ass motherfucker!"

And see white people want to tell us to shut up bad in the movie theater. They want to tell us to shut up bad. But they're scared they're gonna get their ass kicked. So they don't say nothing. They just gesture and shit. And go tell on you and shit. 'Cause them some telling ass motherfuckers.

7

And is it me, but don't some white people get funky with your ass when there's a lot of white people and you're the only black? They get funky with you, don't they? They act like you annoy them and shit. You can't ask a simple question. You can go in a supermarket, there's twenty white people around and you're the only black. You walk in the supermarket. "Hi. How you doing? Excuse me. Can you tell me where I can get some toothpaste from?" "If you look up on six it says. It says toothpaste. You just have to fuckin' read. Toothpaste. Use your vowels." Let a gang of black people ask that same shit: "Excuse me! Can you tell all us where we can get some toothpaste from?" "Sure. I'll show you. Come on. What are you looking for? Colgate Tartar Control, what?" You fuckin' keep that. Huh! Got to get over this racial shit. It's very important, man. We got to be human beings, motherfucker.

TWO

Stay out of jail, black men. Stay out of jail. You know that. You know. There's enough of us in there. It's just sad, man. Better not be a black person in here that says they don't know nobody in jail. 'Cause that's bullshit.

Ray Ray. Earl. Craig. Shorty Tim. All them motherfuckers in jail. The ones that are locked up sending pictures home like jail is a nice motherfuckin' place to be. Always posing, too. Talking about . . . Shit. If I was in jail, my shit wouldn't look like that . . . See, that's why I can't go to jail, man, 'cause I know they're gonna try and fuck me. You know. And how am I gonna tell my mother I've been fucked in jail. "Mama, they fucking me, mama." Well, you know your mama's gonna try and console you. "That's all right, baby, if somebody else put their dick in your ass just lock your ass. Lock it and snap it and break." Snap the shit off. That's why I can't go to jail 'cause I know they're gonna try to rape me. Not 'cause I look good. Just for bragging rights. Just to say, "Oh, Martin? Oh, yeah, I fucked him. He tried to lock on me and shit." You know what I'm saying? I can't handle that. That's why I got my shit planned. If I got to go to jail, see, I ain't gonna wash my ass. See, I'm gonna be a nasty, dirty, filthy, stinky motherfucker.

I'm gonna walk in shit. I'm gonna . . . Oh, I'm gonna wipe my ass with my hand and I'll wave. Come here for a minute. Fuck ya'll. Fuck ya'll, man. Ya'll don't want no ass.

One thing if I have to like anything about jail, 'cause jail is a fucked-up place to be, is that when a brother goes in there and uses his time wisely. You know, pick up a book, you know, read. You know. Don't give a fuck what it is,

Ain't read nothing all their life. Could be *Mary Had a Little Lamb* but they try hard, you know what I said. Mary lame. Hold on. Mary had a little lamb. Mary had a little—how many lambs did the bitch have, man? I'll bet he be checking with your ass from now on before he go to sleep. Excuse me. Look here, do you need something before I go to bed?

No, 'cause you know, fuck that. You can't pause in a black show. Nigger, get your water and hurry the fuck up. Nobody come here to see you drink water, motherfucker.

WOMEN IN AUDIENCE: Martin, we love you.

THREE

My mom's kept me out of jail. My mother and my family kept me out of jail. And I thank my mom's family so much for that, man. My mother's that strong black woman. You know, I love her. And you know what I'm talking about. You love your mother like I do, you know there ain't nothing like a mother, man. Nothing like a mother. Because your mother will back you when no one else will back your ass. Your mother will stay there with you through it all.

You could fuckin' kill somebody, all you got to do is go, "Mama, I had to kill the both of them." Your mother like, "I know. I know. No. He parked in your parking space, there was nothing you could do but kill his ass."

YOU SO CRAZY

13

And see my mother's so cool, man, 'cause she raised six of us. You see, my father was there for a little while, but then they broke up. You know. And I can never—I can understand, you know, sometimes relationships don't work out, your parents don't get along and they break up, your father go his way, but take care of your motherfuckin' kids. It ain't their fault. No. You got to. 'Cause no kid has to be in this world. They don't have to be here. So you got to take care of your kids. And my father left, man, and it was fucked up. Because when he was there, man, we had a yard, ya'll. You know, we was running around in the yard. And then he left and shit, we were like the Jeffersons. Well, we're moving on down. And we were in the projects and shit in the street ducking cars. My mom's this strong black woman say we gonna be all right. And she raise six of us so it was cool.

When he left, though, we didn't really have the money and shit for my mother to do all the things we needed. And my mother, you know, she tried hard. You know, we try to go out and buy some things we want like other kids. You know. We want Nikes, she'd go out and buy Cikes. "Ma, these are Cikes." "All you got to do is paint a damn N on the motherfucker. It's the same damn thing. So what they got heels on them. It's the same damn thing."

So my mom was trying. She tried. We always had a little food in the house but we never really had much food 'cause it was like six of us, and shit, you know. And there was times my mother didn't eat. I said, Mom, why don't you eat something. And she make up an excuse. "I'm on a diet. Y'all kids go and eat." Well, you need to take a bite of this shit, mama. Your stomach's growling. 'Cause I knew she was hungry. You know.

And one thing we always had in the house in the ghetto was bread. Always had some motherfuckin' bread. And if you from where I from, black people know you can do a lot with some good damn bread, can't you? You know what I'm talking about, black people. You remember them motherfucker applesauce sandwiches and shit. Right? Sugar sandwiches. What was the best shit of all of them? The little syrup motherfuckin' sandwiches. You sit on the porch with a syrup sandwich like that. Mama gonna work it out. Mama gonna work it out. Eating a motherfuckin' syrup sandwich.

We was one of those families that wasn't too proud to beg, you know. We go next door 'cause there was days we wanted meat. We ain't had no meat in the house. We go next day, no shame in our gang. We go next door, "Excuse me. Y'all got a pack of hot dogs we can borrow? Y'all got no baloney, no nothing? Well, did y'all get your government cheese yet? Well, fuck y'all. Y'all got some food. I seen y'all go shopping yesterday, motherfucker. That's right, don't come outside I'm gonna bust your head with a loaf of bread." But it's cool though. Mom, she did it—you did a good job, mom.

FOUR

Having fun. All the pretty ladies here. What the fuck is it with the burgundy? I'm saying, are you getting hair to match your shit now? Baby! No! Burgundy hair is not cute. No, it's not. You like one of the Pointer Sisters on crack. I'm just messing with you, babe, what I'm just saying, burgundy hair and shit, who told you to get that? Whoever told you that shit's not your friend. You gonna change that motherfucker now, ain't you? Yeah, come back here have blue hair.

Hi, white people, hi! Didn't see you guys. Thank you for coming out, having the courage, thank you. I know they looking at the TV like, "Oh, fuck, who is the nigger, huh? Why can't we get them banned?

YOU SO CRAZY

17

Fuckin' HBO, letting anybody on. Fuck! Fuck! This freedom of speech shit!"

I fuckin' love being black. Everything we do we smooth with our shit. And you know a lot of white people are watching. Tell 'em. Tell 'em. White people, we proud to be black. That's right. We proud of Kunta Kinte, we all that shit. Everything we do, we walk smooth. Everything we do we just cool. Five do you, motherfucker.

White people can't help it, they're just chipper, just— These guys can't help it. That's why they always taunt you, black people. Watch it, that's how they get you in court. They want you to hit them and shit. "Come on, fuckin' hit me. Fuckin' hit me. Come on. Right fuckin' here." Soon as you hit 'em, bam! "The nigger in the blue hat." But we ain't gonna do that, we ain't going that route. We just cooling. We just happy to fuckin' be here.

Got my man over here, Flavor Flave, look at him, Flavor Flave. I know. Ain't nobody like Flavor Flave. All right, nigger, sit your ass down, this is my show. You can't, Flave, you can't fuck with me on the mike, man. Flave, sit down, man. All right, you crazy, but I'm crazy too, motherfucker. Flave so ugly roaches do like this: "Daddy!"

18

Hey, baby, how you doing? This is your friend. He look nervous. I ain't gonna fuck with you, man. What's your name, man? That's your name? What is your name? What is your name? You shy and shit? What's your name, man, I want to know. 'Cause that's what we gotta do, brothers, we gotta rap to each other.

What's up? Your name Mike? How you living, Mike? You cool. What you do for a living, Mike? Stealing, huh? Mike be walking into stores and shit like this: "What you want, a rib, hon?" No, is this your girlfriend? Man, y'all got some slamming, women, well, everywhere, but y'all some fine motherfuckers, ladies. Y'all know it too. Who you laughing at? You're fine. Sure, 'cause you're Nubian sisters, you know what I'm sayin'? Bit titties, just— you know what I'm saying.

African, that's what I love, my African sister, you know. In Africa, you know, we was there y'all, this was us, in Africa. We was chilling. You know, walking around buck naked. We wasn't afraid of our bodies. When we got over in America they told us we gotta cover our shit up. Ladies, I want to go back to Africa. Pull y'all titties out right now. I know some of y'all ain't gonna pull y'all shit out 'cause you look like raisins. Yo! Girl. Yo! Get ready to go to bed with a girl, titties look like raisins, but you don't want to make her feel bad so you lick the mother fuckers anyway. 'Cause you can't grab with the whole hand, you gotta, two fingers. Oh, shit! Got your ass now. 'Cause I'm a nipple man, myself. You don't have to have much titties, just a nipple.

I'm looking at my sisters, man, beautiful women, man. That's all we think about, though. Brothers could be playing basketball, but pussy is on their mind, always. I gotta foul, nigger. Yo! After this, let's go to the club and get some pussy. That's all we think about is pussy. We gotta get off of that. Start channeling our energies into pussy. Love some pussy. Love making love. Damn right I do. Yo! Boning girl so good, she look back at your ass, I mean with confusion, like who are you? You hitting it, bam! Bam! She turn around like this. Like the name's Reggie.

My man's in the house. Give him a round of applause, my partner. This boy's bad. Wesley Snipes! Real bad motherfucker. You smile at me, motherfucker, don't sit there, playing "New Jack City." What's up, boy? Bad, chocolate motherfucker, ain't him? That motherfucker's too cold. He did some shit in "Jack City" that just made motherfuckers say, "Oh!" Bad motherfucker.

I know you got it good, Wes. Women can't leave your ass now, can they? I bet in the day they used to dog you: "You ain't shit. Get your ass out of here. You little black motherfucker. Get the fuck out of here."

Now you the motherfuckin' man. Now you tell a woman like this, "Get your shit and get out." She like this, "What's wrong with you? I'm said, just horsing me, I mean, you ain't, I mean, why you getting all upset?" It's the American way.

What's up? I see a white section up there. There's a lot of white section. Uh-huh, keep your ass right up there. Now you know how the fuck we felt for years. Hey! Rosie Perez in the house. What's up, Rosie? *White Men Can't Jump*, uh-huh. They can't pump either. You know that shit now, don't you? That's my girl 'cause we go way back. Me and her, first movie together. I love you, baby, you in my heart, what's up?

Yeah! Got Tony Campbell and Oakley from the Knicks and all the brothers in the house from the Knicks. Man, y'all gonna win this shit this year or what? Now stop bullshitting, lose the fuckin' game?

And don't be back there laughing too, man. With the big-ass purple, look like a big-ass grape. Now, Oakley always laughing and playing and fouling motherfuckers. Foul me, I'm telling you, you foul me, I'm like this, "Come on." Just play, Oak, I love you, man. What's happening? What's up, man.

Bubba! Bubba Johnson with the Giants. Got new coach, huh? So that means y'all gonna win three games this year, huh? No, Pepper, my mother, that's my man. Pepper, I can't hang out with you football players. You motherfuckers are crazy when y'all get to drinking. Y'all just be "Fuck!" Scary, huh? What you doing with a vest on? I know you got money, boy, you look good. Ain't he a big good-looking black brother, ain't he? Look at the sisters, they like that. Stand there looking at your wallet. How you doing, Bubba? Bubba Johnson. How you doing with the hairdo? I just want to know about the hairdo. Now, that's your hair, right? Now tell me the truth. Hold on, sister, this is us. You know what I'm saying. We talking to her right now. Mind your motherfuckin' business. Now that's all yours. That's nice, though, who did that? Girl, talk to me, who did your hair? Huh? No, tell the crowd who did it. No, we don't fuckin' know Neecie, who Neecie is? Neecie?

23

Oh, you. How Neecie do your hair and her shit fucked up? I'm joking. Hey! Just playing. Neecie, Neecie, I'm just joking. Chump, leave her hair alone.

My man Kid just bought a house. You know Kid from Kid 'N Play. My man, how did Kid 'N Play get rebirthed. Aren't they Kriss Kross now? Don't be oooing. The motherfuckers just cut their height down. They like, jump, jump, jump, jump. They making money all over. No bullshit. They my boys. Don't look now, Kid, you know I'm fucking with you, man. We did movies together, man. I like y'all, man, you know. But Kriss Kross rolling. And y'all rolling. Y'all should get together and get one big united front. You gonna dog me later 'cause I fucked with you. Kid say, "All right." You mad at me? Well, then, fuck it, Kid, because I've moved on.

FIVE

Yo, y'all seen that shit on HBO, the show on HBO where you confront your killer? Anybody see that shit? Or you confront the person who tried to kill you? HBO, only white people can do that shit. What the fuck do y'all be thinking about, man? White people, "I wanna know why you fuckin' hit me. I gave you the money. All you had to do was leave. Why did you fuckin' keep hitting me?" You know a black man ain't never gonna admit that shit. He's like, "I'm saying, right, early limb head hit you. It wasn't me. Now get the fuck on out my face with that bullshit and get them cameras out of here."

And this gay stuff in the military. Leave gay people alone. Let them do their thing, man. Fuck that. You

YOU SO CRAZY

know what I'm saying, they should be able to fight in the war just like any-fucking-body else. It's their thing, you know, they march and shit. Them good motherfuckin' soldiers, 'cause they emotional with this shit. I bet they coming-home party a motherfucker. No, I'm just saying. You know, a brother wants to get his dick sucked at the airport. Ah, way to go! Watch the gay people get mad at me and start picking at me and writing and shit. Martin, you're an asshole, you're an asshole. It's just a joke, gay people, everybody, everybody should laugh. It's jokes. But them motherfuckers could shut you down, you know, you know that. Them motherfuckers, 'cause they don't leave. They just stand outside your motherfuckin' house. Fuck that shit!

We got some little pretty ladies here. Little light-skinned ladies. Now, you looked mixed. Are you? Yeah, see. You're not black, you're not white, you're confused. Wooo! You're sort of like Kid from Kid 'N Play. I'm just joking.

I always wonder about when people are mixed, like—you know, I was just getting to know why. I was just saying that helps during the riot, 'cause you could just jump on the white side. Fuck 'em, just fuck 'em.

27

Oh, man, hey! Two white guys together. What happened? Computer date fuck up or something, you had to, you kinda had to like, had to like make that shit work. Yo, don't get red and shit, goddamn. I mean, come on, man, fuck, man, I'm just glad you guys here. I get so happy when I see white people come out, they got courage. This is a lot of black people, white people say, "Oh!" And I admire, I'm glad. But how does it feel, you guys know that your rights are protected? How does that feel?

I mean, we just wanna know some things. How does it feel to catch a cab in New York just to go, "Thank you"! How does that feel? Oh, damn!

I tell you, man, the core system in this whole shit is messed up. I was watching this shit, man, Dahmer, that motherfucker, you know, that eating motherfucker. Eating. And they put him on trial. What the fuck is America thinking about? What the fuck is the trial about? You found an ass in his refrigerator. Dicks in the ice tray. Fuckin' ears in the ashtray. What the fuck is the problem?

If that was a black man eating white people, they would've brought the electric chair to his motherfuckin' house. Think about it, man, somebody in society eating another motherfucker. And I really feel sorry for the families that went through that shit. He worked in a goddamn chocolate factory. So that means somebody in this motherfucker had a Snicker with some extra nuts in that motherfucker. Why that's mighty chewy!

What's up, man? Yo! Give my man a round of applause, Jason Williams, play for Philadelphia 76ers. Stand up, man. Don't be fronting me. Look, girls like, "Aaaa, aaaa, oh, girl, he got good hair. Look at his hair, uh-huh, his hair is aaaa. I don't care about what he do, but look at his *hair*."

Jason, you a big motherfucker, man. How tall are you? Six-ten. Dick slinging. Six damn ten. I got on baggy shit and you can fill these mother, can you? I went in the locker room. You brothers don't care, man. 'Cause you know they do interviews naked. They just be there, dick just be like this. So anyway we felt the ball and go—how you will not look at their dick. You like this, "Yeah, uh-huh."

It make me mad, man, 'cause my girl came in there with me. And you know, we went home and made love, I'm like this. She talking about Jason. "Bitch, I ain't no goddamn Jason. Get your ass out this bed." "I didn't mean to say that."

Goddamn. You would just hate to put a rubber

on that, you know, man. No, but you got to, I mean if we get to know each other then maybe I don't have to, but, fellows, use your shit, man, seriously. Use him. Boss like this, he gotta look, "Yeah, you right, boy, you right, 'cause you be burning all that shit, man. Dick fall off. You don't want no white boy running up to you bringing your dick back too." "You dropped your dick about a mile back, man."

I love New York. They, I think we gotta live there, you don't have to say that about us. New York's very nice—just no parking. It's fucked up. Handicapped people got very good parking spaces. I parked there. This is a weird motherfuckin' town. Just steam piss coming out of the ground. I'm not lying. I was walking and I swear to you, there was this brother in the daytime, just pissing, just pissing in the daytime. And the cop told him, "Move over." 'Cause he had to piss too.

Clean up New York and please send money. Clean this motherfucker up. Damn! What do you got here, the street-corner preachers? That's cool. I like that. 'Cause them brothers will always tell you they just got out of jail, always trying to drop knowledge on you.

"Say, little brother, can I speak to you for a minute? You look like you are lost."

"No, I'm going to 125th Street, that's where I'm going. I know where I'm going."

"No, brother, I'm saying, you're lost within your mind. See, when we can rise as a people, and develop our minds and try to get into what we're trying to do, then I think that we can try to do our thing, see. You know what I'm saying? All right? Long time ago, brother, I was incarcerated. They had called me the inmate. You know what I'm saying? That's what I am, okay? I am a prisoner of this system. You know what I'm saying? We got to learn how to grab one another, bring each other up, lift each other up. How can we do that?"

I was like, "All right, shit! How can I do that?"

"Well, for $5.99 I can give you all the knowledge you need."

Let's clean it up. How you doing, brother? 'Cause see, that's how we gotta greet each other, man. I'm saying, brother say, "What's up? What's up? How you doing, partner? How you feel today?" Like that. How come we can't do that? Brothers act like they can't speak to other brothers. What's up, man? Fuckin' with you. Motherfuckin' you are my man.

Women do that same shit. We gotta stop this. Women, you know y'all do that shit. They hate one another, woman come in there. Come into the room. "Look at that bitch." "I'm just saying you do not wear no sandals with a dress, okay? You don't do that, all right?"

White people speak to your ass like a mother, when it's like a lot of black people, won't they speak to you. They're funky when it's like just one black person and there's a whole lot of white, white people get real funky with you. "How you doing there?" "What the fuck does he want?" Then a gang of black people say, "How you doing? Hi, how you doing? Something I can get y'all, something I can take ya? All righty. Fuckin' all righty. Don't want no violence. Just want to love ya." Okay.

How old are you, man? Fifty-five. Fifty-five years old. Don't you love old people? You got to respect them, don't you? They see you dancing, they say, "What's that dance you doing there, boy? Oh, shit, that ain't nothing but the scrawl. That's all that is. That's all that is. You ain't doing no shit we ain't done."

You like, you know, you go to church?

Do you go to church a lot? It's all right. Church

all right, man. Go to church, man, be there. You know. I'm with it. I got baptized when I was young. This is some phoney preachers out there. I hope we can get them out the church, you know, 'cause that's my stuff, you know what I'm saying? That's my stuff. And I think somebody set me up in church 'cause when I was baptized they, you know, you know how you get the Holy Ghost? They take you in that water and they dip you and they say when you come up you know you gonna be talking in an unknown tongue. So when I went to get baptized, they dipped me and came up. I came up. You talking in an unknown tongue. I said, "Fuck you, man, that water cold as shit."

Spike Lee, what's up, man? Oh, you cool, now. Hey! Spike put me in my first movie, *Do the Right Thing*, man. Motherfucker ain't employed me since. What did I do to you, man? Yeah, he always starting trends and shit. Know that shit "Doing the Butt," and he ain't got no ass. Very near broke both legs. Whoa! I'm just fuckin' with you, Spike. I'm just fuckin' with you, man. That's my motherfucker!

SIX

Man, your life changes when you make money.

You can do things when you got money that you can't do when you don't have no money. Man, when you got money you could tell your lady stuff like shut the fuck up.

Hey. And she'll shut up too, won't she? She'll shut up too, won't she? She'll say you're so crazy. But she'll shut up.

You can't shut 'em up if you ain't making no money, man. Especially a black woman. "Wait a minute, motherfucker, you don't tell me to shut up, okay? 'Cause you ain't done a damn thing for me."

Okay. I watch black women get that head going,

man. That's why you can't hit black women. Can't get to that head. "Don't you hit me. Don't you . . . Don't you hit me, motherfucker."

But I'm learning all about relationships, man. I'm learning, learning, big time. Right? I'm finding, boy, women love to get men to cry in relationships. Am I right, ladies? You like that, right?

'Cause you know, if you get that man to cry in that relationship that man's really in love with you. Or you got some good pussy going, all right? Don't think he's crying 'cause you make a helluva ham sandwich.

I ain't never seen no man arguing with a lady, talking 'bout, girl, I should leave your ass, girl, I should, the way you put that mayonnaise on that ham there? Fuck that. No. No. I'm gonna hang in there. I'm gonna hang in there.

Yo. You ever had some good pussy and just start crying? You know, 'cause you overwhelmed that it's so good. You're in the motherfucker and you like, "This is some good pussy, baby."

What kind of pussy is this?

Häagen Dazs? You got almonds in that motherfucker?

That's a fuckin' almond.

That is a fuckin' almond, baby. Can you change that shit over to chocolate chip? Oh, that's really my favorite.

Yeah, man, 'cause it's good, man. That's why they love to get you to cry. I think it's easier to get out of a relationship with a white woman than it is with a black woman. 'Cause a white woman you could just—white guys just go to 'em, "Honey, I don't feel it no more. Goddamn it, you heard me, I don't feel it no more, I want out the fuckin' relationship. I want out."

And a white woman'll just say, "Okay, Bob, if you want out of our goddamn relationship I'll see your ass in court. Good-bye."

Not with no sister. You go to her, "Yo, baby, uh-uhm, I don't really feel that shit no more, I want out of the relationship, it ain't gonna work." Black woman go off, "You want out of what? Halla halla halla halla halla halla halla. Halla halla halla halla. No, motherfucker, we will work this shit out."

The guy get all scared, "All right, baby. Shit, we'll work it out."

You know what kills me, though, in relationship? Guys that act like they can't cry. They think they a sucker if they cry. No, man, if it hurts, let it out, man. The guys that hurt . . . the ones that try to hold it in. You can't hold that shit in, man. But guys try anyway.

Women could come to us, "Look, you don't respect me, you don't respect the relationship, I am leaving you, good-bye."

Men are like, "So, if you're gonna leave, leave. Get the fuck out. I'm gonna be all right. I'm a man, I'm gonna be all right. You a trip. You like this shit, Tina, you like to see me fuckin' cry, right? Damn, girl, yeah, that's what you want to see, you want to see little tears out of my eyes, right? Drip drop, drip drop. You like that shit. I love the shit out of you, woman. I should crack your fuckin' forehead. 'Cause I'm sayin' I might not be the best man in the world, but last Christmas I spent a lot of shit on you. All my money went to you, girl. What, I bought you a hat, a scarf, a T-shirt, I want all of my shit back."

Don't take the stuff back that you buy them, though. Don't take that back. Take your shit back that you own. 'Cause if not it'll be another man around when you leave wearin' your shit, wearin' your bedroom slippers.

"Oh, these a real motherfuckin' nice here. The boy even wore my size."

You know what I'm finding, though? I'm finding there's women in relationships that they don't want to be in no more. It's not that you don't want to leave the guy, it's just you can't, 'cause that motherfucker is crazy and deranged. And he won't let you go nowhere. Am I right? But you try, you know, you try to get out of the relationship. You go to him, "Excuse me, could I talk to you for a minute?"

He like, "Uh-huh, what the fuck you want to talk about? Huh? It better not be about nobody leaving, 'cause there ain't nobody leaving no-fuckin'-body. Better not be about that shit."

Woman gets scared, "I just playing, you want a ham sandwich or something?"

"I sure do, put cheese on it."

Yo, I heard one guy 'cause he's jealous and possessed—I heard one guy tell his lady, "You try to leave me I'm gonna kill me, you, and the dog."

The dog was like, "Yo, I ain't got shit to do with this, man. You motherfuckers better stop arguing, man."

The dog was scared. Yo. 'Cause you dating that jealous, possessive man. If he ain't treating you right, leave that motherfucker. Don't stay with him, he ain't right.

He don't even want to see you go out with your girlfriends and have a good time, do he? He don't want to see you go out. Motherfucker come in the club looking for your ass. "Where the fuck, I tow her ass. Get your shit, let's get the fuck out of here."

And her girlfriends like, "Know what he did?"

And you got to play straight: "No, he ain't mad, I had told him that I was gonna, but look, I gotta get ready to go, I told him."

'Cause you know he gonna whip your ass. I mean, 'cause he's so jealous and he's possessive. He accuse you of shit you ain't even doing. You can't even watch cartoons without him accusing you of something. You know, you're sitting around the TV, eating cereal, or since we're black people, you know what I'm talking about, cereal. He get mad, you're looking at this cartoon, he get mad. You just sitting there laughing, aha ha ha. And he get mad.

"You want to fuck Barney Rubble, don't you? You like Barney, huh? You think he's special 'cause he could stop a car with his feet, huh? You like that shit, huh? Girl, I knock your head off, right."

And then they have the woman talking all crazy. She be on the phone with her girlfriend crying, "Oh, no, girl. He—oh, I don't know what his problem—he accuse me of wanting to go to bed with Barney Rubble, girl. But, but . . . but I don't even know where Bedrock is. I got to go, girl, I think he gonna want a ham sandwich, I call you back. Bye."

Leave him. Leave him. You know who you are. 'Cause you're sitting right next to that man right now. You're crying out, you're sitting next to him, going, "Help me."

Leave him. 'Cause if you don't leave him, it starts turning into him hitting on you and beating you. And that's what you don't want. That's what you do not want. But check it out. Some women are so dumb they stick with the mother who beat their ass. I can't see it. I saw a woman last week, all fucked up. I said, "Your man hit you, didn't he?" She said, "Yeah, but he say he love me, though."

I said, "That ain't love, baby, that ain't love." She said, "Yeah, he say he love me. He gonna take me to Hawaii and we gonna watch the sun come up as soon as I can open my eyes."

I said, "I hope your ass see blue water. Gotta leave him."

Some of 'em will—But I tell you, jealous white guys, they do just weirder—they do weirder shit. Don't they? When you read about it in the paper, white guys, they cut their lady's head off and put it in the 'frigerator and shit. And talk to it every day. "Goddamn it, don't ever cheat on me. Don't ever cheat on me. I'm talking to you." The head's going . . . "Until you know how to answer me . . . I'll be back."

Treat your lady right, guys, that's all I ask. 'Cause I'll fuck your lady. That's right. Your lady be over my house crying, saying, "My man don't know how to treat me." I be like what?

Turn around, baby, turn around. See, he got to learn to respect you. That's what that's all about.

She be like this: "You understand me, though."

I sure do. I sure do. Ladies, make sure it's over with your man before you go running to somebody else, that's why I say that. 'Cause there's men that's waiting to hear your stories. "Come on in, come on in."

But you got some women who don't play: they will kill your ass. That's why they say don't argue with your lady and go to bed mad, they will fuck you up and whip your ass.

I was arguing with my lady the other night. I went to sleep. And I woke up about four A.M. in the morning and she wasn't in bed and it was dark in the house, I couldn't see shit. And I said, feeling in my bed, and I said, "Ba-ba-baby? Baby, where are you?" And I just heard her voice say, "Hush up, stop making all that noise." I said, "What you doing?" She said, "I got up to go to the bathroom. Go on back to sleep." I said, "Well, if you got up to go to the bathroom why don't you have on any lights?" She said, "I don't need no lights to go to my bathroom. Go on back to sleep." So I got ready to lay back down.

Just out of curiosity I jumped up and cut on a light. Bitch had lighter fluid in her hand and every damn thing else.

Talking about "I was gonna cook." I ain't asked for shit to eat.

I tell you, man, they're crazy. They will burn you up; they will kill you. But I find there are some women that get jealous. Like they don't want to hear shit about your ex-girlfriend. If that shit is supposed to be over, let it be over.

Yo, guys, you could go to them crying about your ex-girlfriend, you could go to them fuckin' crying and they don't want to hear. You run to them, "Oh, baby, you remember my ex-girlfriend, Sheron, oh, damn. She was in a car accident today, baby. Oh. She's in the hospital, she's in critical condition, she's unconscious, they don't know if she's gonna make it, baby. Woman like this!"

"She in critical condition? . . . She unconscious, huh?"

"Yeah, yeah, yeah, baby, look here. I'm gonna hurry up and go over to the hospital to see what's going on."

Woman get mad, "Hold on, wait a minute, motherfucker, hold up. Didn't you hear what you just told me? You said she is unconscious and she's in critical condition. Why the fuck are you gonna go over there for, she ain't gonna know if you're there?"

Huh? See that bitch thinks she's slick.

They're crazy, man. They will kill you. Know what's something though? One time, a woman told me: "If you leave me I think I'll kill myself." Yeah, right. Come on, if you want to die, right, there's some surefire ways you can do it.

One morning we got in a real bad argument. I said, "Hell with you, woman." And I stormed out of the house. I got home late that afternoon, she's sitting in the middle of the floor with a razorblade in her hand. I said, "Oh my goodness, woman, what are you doing?" She said, "You lucky you caught me. I was just about to kill myself."

I said, "Bitch, you had all day to kill yourself. Should be dead by now." I didn't do the dishes, man, I was mad as hell.

The whole day gone. She gonna pick up the razorblades. "You want a ham sandwich?" "Yeah, but not with that razor."

SEVEN

I'm fucking amazed how women like motherfuckers with good hair. I don't know what that shit is. Man, my sister is married to a motherfucking convict. She married him 'cause he had good hair. I told her, "What the fuck are you doing?" She said, "Uh-uh, you don't understand. That motherfucker love me." I said, "What the fuck you mean?" "Uh-uh, I'm gonna tell you so, that motherfucker got some good ass hair." But, let me tell you, we see black people we don't like with good hair we always make some goddamn excuse, don't we? You know, say, "Excuse me, damn baby, you got some, that's your hair?" She say, "Yeah, that's all me." Say, well, "Damn, that's real pretty, got nice hair." "Uh-uh, well, you know, we got Indian in our family." Get the fuck out of here.

I hate a pretty motherfuckin' woman. 'Cause they're hard to leave, man. You know what I'm saying, you can't walk out on the motherfuckers right. You know, "What? Well, then fuck it, if you can't understand me, fuck it! Hey! Shit! Why you doing this to me?" That shit is hard.

EIGHT

If you're living at home, you know, with your mother in the basement, you're too grown for that shit. Get up off the ass. If you're a grown adult, especially a man thirty-five years old, at home putting your name on the orange juice. Talking about, "Ma, don't touch my shit."

Get out of the basement, man, 'cause I'm gonna tell you what's gonna happen. Your mother's gonna come in the basement catch some girl down there sucking your dick. Then you all gonna be embarrassed. Your mother walk in, "Ah!" You like, "Ma?" Your mother, "I didn't see nothing. I didn't see nothing." But most of all the girl sucking your dick is embarrassed. "Oh, my God! Your mother caught me

YOU SO CRAZY

sucking your dick! Your mother caught me. I got to go apologize to your mother." Girl go upstairs, "Miss Lawrence? Oh, Miss Lawrence, I'm so sorry you caught me sucking your son's dick in your house. Miss Lawrence, I'm so sorry." But you know your mother gonna back you. "That's all right. That's all right. Just stop letting his balls drag. It's cold in the basement, okay? Pick the balls up. Cup the balls."

Some of you ladies know what I'm talking about? You remember when you first met the man. He come up to you in a club and he was the nicest motherfucker you could meet. A gentleman. He walk up to you in a club, woo, shit.

"Excuse me. Hello. How you ladies doing. Umm, I was about to leave the club. I feel real embarrassed 'cause I know you ladies are doing your thing, but I was about to leave the club and, umm, your beauty just like, bam, stopped me like that. Umm, can I leave my card, and if you don't have a man, I hope you use it. Listen, ladies, I'm sorry I interrupted you guys. Girl, you're as lovely as you want to be. Bye-bye. Take it easy."

And then the girls are like, "Ah! God, that was nice! Oh, don't no man ever come up to us like that.

That was real nice. You ain't seen no signs of him being crazy. Deranged."

So one day you walking around looking at this card. You know, I am so tired of men's bullshit. You know, maybe I'll call him, see how he acts. So, you dial the phone. "Hello. Can I speak to Reg? Oh, hello?" "Yeah. Yeah, this is Reg." Umm, this is Debbie. I met you at the club. I was with my girlfriends and the one you said as lovely as you want to be." "Oh, yeah, hey! How you doing? Girl, I'm so glad you called me. I'm so glad you called. Uh, I guess that means you don't have a man." "Well, I'm single, right now, but I was calling to tell you I was a little impressed with how you came up. I mean, no man ever did that. I thought that was very nice." "Hey, well, I got to be me. Well, I'm kind of busy all week and I was wondering if you would like to get together tonight or is it the last minute?" "What? Oh, no. No. This is perfect. Because I wasn't doing nothing, you know, just laying here watching Andy Griffith, you know. But, uh—uh—uh, let me wash my hands and, uh, get a pen, get your address. I'll come get you."

So you hang the phone up. You go call your girl. "Girl, he's on his way over. He sounds so nice on the

51

phone. He sound just like he did that night. Girl, I hope this is the one for me. Good-bye." Now, you ain't heard nothing on the phone of him being crazy. Deranged. So he come pick you up, y'all go out to dinner. Everything's kicking at dinner. Lovely. Everything's nice and beautiful. You're looking at each other. The way you smile, the way you move.

"Girl, you something else." "I've been hurt a lot." "Yeah, well, I have, too." "Got a little something on your mouth. Damn, will you look at the time? It's almost twelve. You know what? I don't even want to keep you out too late, so let me get you home. I would like you to get some rest so you can hopefully think about me tomorrow."

So he gets you home, right? Right at twelve. And you like, "Damn! This is very nice. No man ever really got me home at twelve. They like to keep me out all night." "Hey, I'm not like every man."

So you close the door, you call your girlfriend. "Girl! Oh! Girl! Girl, this motherfucker came pick me up." You tell her about the date. "And he was so nice. Girl, he didn't even want to keep me out all night. Wiping food off my mouth, girl. I mean, he looked so good in his little suit. I mean, he had on some white sweatsocks, but, I mean, I could change that. I could change him. You ain't seen no side of him being crazy. Deranged." Now you spend a lot of time with him. About three months, right? And one day your girls decide to come over because they ain't been spending no time with you. "Girl, what's up? Why don't you go out with us tonight?" And you're like, "Girl, I've been spending a lot of time with my man. He's been good to me. I have the perfect man." "Well, if he's such a good man, he understand it's all right for you to hang out with your girls every now and then. I mean, did you ask him could you go out? I mean, you know how men are about us going out. They don't like us to go nowhere." And you're like, "You right. I never did ask him to find out see how he is about that. Wait a minute. Let me go see how he acts. I might be going with y'all."

"Baby, umm, I know we were supposed to spend a lot of time together today and everything, but my girls, I haven't been out with them for a while. Do you mind if I go with them? I mean, what's up?"

"Oh? Oh? You want to go out with your girls? Okay, sure. Go have a good time. I don't—can I stay here? I'm gonna watch TV. Everything gonna be cool. Is that all right? "Okay." "Yeah." "Okay. Fine. Go have a good time."

YOU SO CRAZY

53

And you like, "Ah! girl, yes." And you go out and you have a good time.

Now you ain't seen no sign of him being crazy. Deranged. Now let a couple of months go by and try that same go-out shit. 'Cause one day he call you. "Look here, girl, on my way over. Getting ready to leave work. Getting ready to head over there now." And you're like, "No. No, baby, don't do that. Didn't you get my message? Umm, I'm going out with the girls tonight 'cause we had a little good time last time we was out and I'm gonna go out. You need to stay home and get some rest because last night you just looked so tired, all right? So I got to go. Bye."

And he like, "Hold on. Hold on a minute. What? What? Why the fuck you got to be going out all the goddamn time? Why the fuck you got to keep running to the clubs all the motherfuckin' time? A real lady will keep her ass home sometimes!" You look at the phone. Uh-uh. Click. Hang up on him.

Go in the closet, put on your fuck-'em dress. Go to the club, fuck 'em, girl. Fuck 'em. Fuck 'em, girl. Fuck 'em. Fuck 'em, girl. Fuck 'em. Now, why you in the club saying motherfuck 'em in your fuck-'em dress, you know, you ain't thinking you hung up on a crazy, deranged motherfucker.

So who come walking in the club in their pajamas? "I told her motherfuckin' ass don't hang the phone up on me. Not now, partner, talk to you in a minute. I kill everybody up in this motherfucker. Gonna hang up on me? Look here, woman, get your shit. Let's go...."

Now you got to play this shit off. "No, he not mad. I told him I was gonna meet him. Look, I got to go! I'll call y'all. Bye."

You chasing behind him . . . "All I had was a cooler." He mad as hell getting in the car. Driving. Mad. 'Cause you hung up on him.

Pissed. He like this driving with some footies on.

"I told your ass don't ever play me like that or do me like that." You in the car like this. Shit. The windows are fogging up. You nervous as hell. So you writing HELP on the window and shit. You get in the house, your phone ringing off the goddamn hook. Who is it? It's your girlfriends. "Girl, what the fuck was all that about him embarrassing you in front of everybody?" What do you do? Make an excuse for his crazy, deranged ass. "I know he's not mad. See, umm, last week somebody had got shot down at the club and he was worried that they was gonna get to shooting this week and he didn't want me to get hit. But he said he's sorry and I'll call y'all. Bye."

YOU SO CRAZY

55

Now, you know if a motherfucker is crazy enough to go get your ass out of a club in pajamas, the shit don't get no better. It don't. 'Cause then you ain't gonna talk to each other the same. The communicating. He's mad. You're pissed. You ain't working out. And see, women don't like to leave the relationship because—they go, "Uh-uh. Fuck that. I put too much into this shit." And so women say, "Can we talk?" And he like, "Fuck that. I ain't trying to talk right now. Uh-uh. We ain't got nothing to talk about right now."

'Cause see, men want to talk when we want to talk, and women want to talk when they want to talk. So maybe one day he's sitting in there watching the game. And you say to yourself, Let me go watch the game with him. Maybe that will calm him down. So he's in there watching the game. And everything—keep in mind everything you've done in this relationship up to this point you've annoyed him. You know. He even introduce you differently to people. "This, uh—tell them your name. Tell them your fuckin' name." I'll explain it to you, man.

So one day he's sitting in there, you know, watching basketball. You say, If I go in there, spend some time with him, get involved in what he's doing, maybe we'll communicate and talk about it. So he's in there watching TV. You come to the door. "Excuse me, baby." "What? What?" "Do you mind if I come in to watch the game with you?" Look, if you want to come in, come in close the door. But you got to be quiet. I'm watching the Knicks. You're gonna have to fuckin' be quiet. Can you move over. Now, I don't want you sitting too close, 'cause if I get to swinging elbows, shit, 'cause I might jump up on a good play. Just back up off me a little bit."

"Damn! Why you being so mean lately and acting and everything? I mean, what happened to the guy I first met at the club?" "I don't know." "Is that the Chicago Bulls and the New York Knicks?" "Yeah, that's the Chicago Bulls and the New York Knicks. Sshh!" "Is that Scotty Pippin?" "Who you think it is. Who the fuck do you think it is? What does it say on the back of his jersey? Pip-pin. Pip-pin." "Well, I don't know. It could have been Otis Pippin, I don't know." "Shit." "What's the score?" "Baby, if you wait a minute, they show the score like every two seconds. Damn! She don't know a fuckin' thing about basketball." Foul! I'm saying Charles Smith didn't have to hit him that hard. "Baby?" "What?" "Is that Michael Jordan?" "Goddamnit!" Is that Michael Jordan? Why do you ask dumb, shit, dumb-ass questions? Is that Michael Jordan? You see he's in the fuckin' air."

Now, you know if the motherfucker's going all over you while you trying to do what he like to do, it don't get no better. 'Cause then he gonna start accusing your ass, and shit, you know, jealousy start to sink in.

And you walking down the street one day, he go off. "What the heck does your ass keep click-clacking for when you're walking down the street? Why you got to click-clack, click-clack, clack-clack, clack every time we walking down the goddamn street?" And you like going, "That's just how I walk. I didn't know my ass click-clacked." "Well, the motherfucker keeps click-clacking." Now you got to get a fucked-up walk so your ass don't click-clack. "Is it still click-clacking?" "Yeah."

That's when you know it's time to leave that shit. 'Cause the next thing that come, you gonna try to leave him and the threats come. "Uh-uh. Uh-uh. You try to leave me, I'm gonna tell you somebody's gonna be hurt. I ain't the only motherfucker that's gonna get hurt if you leave me."

That's when you got to take your gun and start—

see, you done lost it at this point. You just got to
... and you got to hope you hit the motherfucker in
the spine, at least. 'Cause you don't want to kill him,
but shoot him in the spine. 'Cause if that motherfucker's gonna stalk you, he gonna stalk your ass in a
wheelchair. He'll be rolling in the clubs and shit like
this. "You seen Debbie? Tell her I'm looking for
her..."

Now what could possibly be worse than a man
being jealous, crazy, deranged? What's worse than
that? A jealous, crazy, deranged woman. 'Cause, see,
they can kill your ass and get away with it.

They can fuck you up and get away with it. Now
see, you don't know when you first meet them,
'cause, you know, you meet this woman, she's doing
everything for you. Cooking. Cleaning. You know,
and you're like, "Damn, girl, you know, you are
something else. I mean, the things you do for me.
You just cook and clean and everything. All the
other women used to have a problem with that."
"Well, I'm not like every other woman." Oh, you
sure as hell ain't like them women. Goddamn.

See, one day that shit gonna come out. 'Cause she
gonna say, "Look, baby, you look a little tired. I
mean, you look like you just don't want to be in the

YOU SO CRAZY

house. Why don't you go out and hang with your friends? Have a good time. Go to the club or something?"

"Wait. Wait. Wait. Wait a minute, now. Let me get this shit straight. You want me to go out and go to the club? Have a good time?"

"Yes. Go out and have a good time at the club with your friends."

"This is! God! See, this is a trip. 'Cause, see, no woman ever just told me to go on and go out and have a good time. Girl, you all right. See, I knew you was the one for me."

You ain't seen no signs of her being crazy, deranged. But see, don't make the mistake and tell her what time you'll be in. 'Cause you get happy.

"Okay, well, shit. I'll be in at twelve o'clock. Okay. I'll see you at twelve." "Remember, I'm not like every other woman." "You sure as hell ain't."

Now, you done told this woman you'd be in at twelve. Let your ass get in at twelve-o-five. You walk in the house, you like this. . . . All the lights are out and shit. And all you hear is "Where the hell have you been? Who the fuck is that? Who was that? What was that?" She comes walking out of the dark with knives around her. "Where the fuck you been?" "Baby, why you fuckin' bugging with knives and shit all around. What's wrong with you?" "Where the fuck have you been?" "I was at the club, babe." "You wasn't at no goddamn club, cause I called the fuckin' club!" "Baby, I don't know what the fuck is wrong. I'm not like every other man." "And you told me you'd be home at twelve." "Baby, I had to walk up the fuckin' steps. It took me five minutes to get up the steps." Now, when a crazy woman gets to doing this shit, pacing, right? Like this and the hand moving, move the fuck out the way. 'Cause she's about to whoop your ass . . . And you know that fight you get in when you're trying to hold each other. You holding her down. Well, she already done fucked you up when she was up.

Where does she scratch your ass when she's whooping your ass? On the face, the neck, and the back. You run out of the house, bleeding, over to your boy's house. . . . Your boy see all this blood. He's like, "Wait a minute. Let me get my shit. You been rumblin' with some brothers?" Wait. You like, "No, man. Calm down. She fucked me up." Now, you stay in this relationship, right? So much this woman gets to whoopin' your ass, your boy gets tired of it. He approach her with some shit. "You know

YOU SO CRAZY

what. That's a good motherfucker. You know, you gonna stop hurting that motherfucker like that. He trying to be right with you." She like this. "Mind your punk-ass business."

A jealous woman, a crazy, deranged woman, hates to see another woman smile at her man. She will embarrass your ass in a restaurant, won't she? She'll pull you aside, "Come here, motherfucker. Come here. Come here."

"What the fuck was all that shit about? The bitch . . . smiling all in your goddamn face."

You like, "No, baby, see that was the coat-check girl. She took my coat and she said, "Thank you, have a nice day."

"Oh, so you don't know the bitch?"

"Baby, calm down. We in a restaurant."

"Fuck! I don't give a fuck where we are! You my man and I can ask you any fuckin' thing I want! Mind your own goddamn business! This is my man! So you know the bitch?"

"I do not know her."

"Oh, you don't know her? You don't know her?"

"Baby, I do not know the girl."

" 'Cause if you want to be with the bitch, you can be with the bitch."

"Babe, I don't know her."

"Oh, so you don't know her? 'Cause I go there and I'll ask the bitch. I'll confront her."

"Baby, that's the coat-check girl."

"No, fuck this shit! Excuse me. Yeah, you, miss. Smiling . . . Yes. I notice you've been smiling all night. I mean, that man down there, do you know him? Who that guy?"

"No, I don't."

"Well, what's all this shit? I mean, what's all that shit about?"

"Ma'am, all I said was 'Thank you have a nice day.'"

"Well, let me tell you something, Miss Thank-You-Have-a-Nice-Day, your job is to check coats. Check 'em, bitch. You bring your ass on over here."

NINE

I love being in love, you know. I think we all do, right? How do you know when you're in love? We ask ourself, you say we do stupid shit. But my definition of that is you know when you're in love when women start walking in the bathroom while you're shitting.

Right? 'Cause, they will kick the bathroom door open just to ask you, boom, "You love me?" You like this, "Yeah, baby, I love you a whole lot, why?" "Just want to know, motherfucker, just want to know."

'Cause when they love you they can walk in the bathroom while you shitting, and smell—and know it's stink in there and act like they don't smell the shit.

'Cause that's love. 'Cause when you're in love you do shit that you didn't do when you first met her. Remember when you first met her, if you ever fart, you run outside, I got to change the tire. I'll be back. But once you get used to it, you fart in their face, brrrrtttt. "Shut up. Make me a ham sandwich."

TEN

Did any—did anybody see the movie *The Fly*? With Geena Davis and Jeff Goldblum? Was that some love for your ass? Only white people could do that, though. White people are amazing. Remember the fly was all fucked up?

And they was rapping, right? And his ear fell off. She hugged him on the side his ear fell off on. She said, "Oh, god, don't worry, I'll hang in there with you, I love you, goddamnit, I'll hang in there." But he couldn't hear 'cause the ear just fell off. He said, "Come to the other side, I can't hear shit."

Now listen, don't get me wrong. I love my lady, y'all. I love her. But if we rapping, and her ear fall off . . . she ain't gettin' no fuckin' hug. We be holdin' hands like a mother, goin' walk with me, just walk. I'm gonna get you to the hospital. I'll put her ear in the pocket, just come on. The ear be in the pocket, jumpin' and shit. Damn, baby, it got the nerves in it, don't it? But that was love for your ass. And look, every time the white woman came back, that's why you all are so amazing, every time the white woman came back he was more and more fucked up.

You remember, and he would throw up on shit, you know, and it was like an acid. You know, and he was just like oouuhh. And the woman it didn't faze her. She, she'd just walk in, "Oh, god, you're changing more and more each day."

And he would like, "I know, damn. I don't know what went wrong. Excuse me. I'm sorry. I'm losing my body, shit. I'm slowly losing my mind." He say, "You gonna have to leave me, because I may, you know, do something to you that I don't want to do because I'm losing my mind."

White woman, "No. I won't leave you. Goddamn it, because I love you and I'm gonna hang every step of the way with you."

You wouldn't have to tell no black woman that.

Black woman would've walked in that house. "Look at your head. Look at your fuckin' head. Uhm, we ain't gonna make it.

"Well, all right, okay, well, you the fly, fly the fuck on out of here now. Fly, motherfucker."

A black woman would put your ass out, man. Get your shit and get out. And I could see her putting the fly out. And she take all his shit and put it in a knapsack and put it on that wing or back or whatever. And say, "Now get the fuck out." Black woman say, "I don't give a fuck what love is, get your ass and get out."

But she put him out a little too soon, 'cause he can't fly yet.

So the motherfucker, he goes to the bus stop. 'Cause he can't fly. So he waitin' at the bus stop. He start gettin' impatient and shit. Start lookin' for the bus.

And so while he waitin' at the bus stop, his lady and her girlfriends drop by in a car. And they say, "Girl, ain't that your man?" Girl say, "Yeah, man, that's him. Shit, he'll never throw up on this pussy."

But I could see the girl at a party, trying to get her life together. You know, she at a party trying to get over the fly.

And he'd show up at the party. Knockin' on the door, right? Bang, bang, bang, bang. And the dude open the door and say, "Ahhhh. Who you want, man?" He like this, "Could you tell Tina to come here for a minute?"

So, so the dude go in there and Tina dancing and shit, having a good time. And the dude go, "Tina, there's this motherfucker out there that . . . Is he all fucked up and everything?"

"Would you tell him that I said it is over and do not come back here no more. Thank you." So Slim go out there, "Yo, man, she said the relationship over, don't come back here no more." He get mad. "Fuck that bitch, man. Tell her ass I could fly now anyway. Fuck it."

I love makin' love, I just love it.

Making love, having sex, whatever you want to call it. We'll do anything for women when we want to go to bed with y'all. Won't we? Do anything. And women get it when we want it most. Like when we're laying in bed butt naked, shit about to happen, am I right? And you say, "Baby, let's do this." She go, "Hold it. I'm thirsty. I know it's not the right time. I know 7-Eleven is three miles away. But would you run and get me something to drink please?" Being the men that we are, "Baby, what you want? Big Gulp, Super Gulp, I got a dollar in my pocket, what you want? Excuse me." We get up, put on some

clothes, run three miles to get 'em a Big Gulp. My lady want a Big Gulp, I'll get her a Big Gulp. 'Cause I'm gonna tear that ass up when I get back.

Am I right? Now we get back, make love to 'em, everything they want it to be. Now we got power, guys, 'cause they, "Ooh, lord, have mercy, that was so good. . . . Would you run in the kitchen and get me a drink of water?" Men got the typical answer, "Shit, you better lick that ice in that Big Gulp, man, I'm goin' to sleep."

But you know as well, we think—damn. We think we hurt women when we make love to 'em. We do. We always talk shit. Women have nine-pound babies falling out of there, man. We ain't doing shit to it, man. We sitting there talking about I'll kill you. She's like "Right, motherfucker, oochie, ouch. Oochie the fuck ouch. Hah."

They do, man. We ain't hurting 'em, man. But women will let you know, though, if you do hurt 'em. That, you know, if you're in the wrong place or you're hurting 'em, you know. "I'm sorry, man, you're in the wrong place." They'll tell you, "Ouch, motherfucker, that ain't it. Out, that ain't it, motherfucker. Well, cut on the lights I'll show you where you need to be. Don't be drilling no holes, all right?"

YOU SO CRAZY

But they will let us know, right. But we guys won't say shit when they're hurting us. You know what I'm talking about; when they on top of you. Billing your dick all fucked up. You be in a hospital with a broke dick. "It was good, doctor, it was good, man. Can you get it on for me?"

I love sex. Ain't no secret. Everybody know I likes to fuck a little bit. I ain't gonna lie. Like to get me a little bit every now and then. Just a little bit. But it's sad though, man, 'cause you can die 'cause of that shit today. Ain't that sad? You can't just be running around boning like you want to. You stick your dick in something and you walk and pass out. But it's wild 'cause you can get with a woman that you wanted for years, man. She laying in bed, titties kicking, pow. Ass, plat, pow. Legs, thighs, just ready, like hurry on it. And you're like, "Yeah, I'm gonna."

And then she cough and shit. "Look, gotta get to work. I'll call you. I'll call you tomorrow. I got to think about this shit." But you know, I use them condoms. I know you don't wanna use 'em, it's hard, it's hard to get up and look for a fuckin' condom, your dick go down or somethin', I know. They catch your hair and shit. You get 'em out, you roll 'em motherfuckers down, they catch your hair and then you can't get the roll back to get the hair out, so you wind up just snatching the mother-fucker and snatch a bald spot out your shit. And the girl's like this, "Huh-huh, what's the bald spot? What's the bald spot? What the fuck is the bald spot? You got the mange or somethin', what the fuck? What the fuck?" It's hard, you know. Especially in the morning, man. It's hard to get out of bed in the morning and go look for a condom put the shit on. Uh-uh. 'Cause in the morning you just want to turn over and get to fuckin', right? You just want to make love in the morning 'cause that's your best time sometimes to fuck. You wake up, you got sleep all in your eye looking all ugly, you know, slob right here, you looking ugly. She looking ugly. Your voice all groggy.

"Good morning to you. I said good morning to you. What you feel like doing this morning?" She sound like you? "What you feel like doing this morning? Let's get it on." See, that's your best fuckin' in the morning sometimes. You know why? Because the pussy marinates at night. The pussy simmers at night. And at six A.M. ding, I'm ready. I know you are.

And the pussy is amazing, isn't it? It's so good. Woo! Isn't pussy delicious? It is—oh! I don't know if

you ladies know how good your shit is. Oh, man, it's amazing, too. It can like—it adjusts. I don't know. It like—it expands and shit. You could throw a chair in that motherfuckin' thing. That's why I be trying to tell my brothers, when you're running from the cops, don't hide in no fuckin' closet, hide in the pussy. Just say, "Look here, baby, I need to get into your pussy for a minute. I'll explain it to you later." "Craig, what you doing here, man?" And you know there'll be some smart cop that's gonna find your ass, right? Some Columbo kind of motherfucker. Ma'am, we got a reason to believe you're hiding someone in the pussy. Why would you say that, officer? 'Cause there's a goddamn Nike hanging out of your pussy.

ELEVEN

Brothers braggin' on your dicks out there. Stop it, bro'. Stop braggin' on your dicks. Stop it. I'm gonna let the world know. I ain't packin'. I'm gonna fuck—I got no big dick. I don't give a shit what you think about me. You know what I'm sayin'? I ain't got no big dick. I ain't packin'. I was not blessed with a big dick. But I, hey, hey, I'll work it with what I have. That's what you gotta tell 'em when you got a little dick and shit. Before you go in the room, "Hey, hey, hey, wait a minute. Look. You're not into anyone hurtin' you, are you? 'Cause that's not gonna happen." 'Cause I ain't gonna lie.

Hey, my dick ain't out here. I see brothers doin' this shit all the time. "My shit down to here, man."

My shit ain't out there. I got a short dick. A short, thick dick. Yeah, I'm a thick-dick nigger. I won't choke you but you get a mouthful.

What happens to your dick when you get out the pool? I know the brothers ain't sayin' nothin'. You know who you are. That mother-fucker is gone, man. Or it's like, fucked up, shriveled up, some kinda way. It's swollen at the head. Look like somebody kicked it in the back. One time I thought I lost my shit. "I lost it." I called 911. "I can't find my dick. I just got out the pool." And, you know, they came over and, "No, man, it's right here." It's like, I thought that was my navel. Brothers—we do this shit a lot. We put our hands in our shit and we always fuckin' with our dicks. We always just holdin' the jugglin' balls, fuckin' around. You ever thought you lost a ball? Ain't that the scariest shit, 'cause you rubbin' your shit and you're like, "Ahh, ahh, I lost my ball." But the mother-fucker in the other sack.

If you're a little-dick motherfucker, you shouldn't ever overplay your stroke. You ever overplay your stroke? Knowin' if you're a little-dick motherfucker, you 'sposed to be in one place, right here, like this. Just one place. But sometimes we think we got room to play with this shit—and us little-dick motherfuckers always fall out. But we cover it up real quick. We like, "Damn, girl, you're wetter than a motherfucker. You wet as shit, girl." And then we try to put it back in and hit the wrong hole. A sister'll tell you, "Huh-huh, huh—that ain't it. That ain't it, motherfucker, that ain't it. Well, put on the goddamned lights. Clap on, clap on, motherfucker. Clap 'em on. You ain't got to get up, I got clap on. Clap it on. Clap on, motherfucker, clap on."

And there's some ugly dicks out there too. I'm sure there's a couple of—Huh? How do I know? 'Cause I wasn't always circumcised, motherfucker. Shit, I got circumcised at like fourteen so I know what it look like for the dick not be circumcised, you know. Now I got my shit circumcised. Look good. I found out on the road trip. Ask your mother am I circumcised. Ask that bitch that. Motherfucker, my dick is circumcised 'cause I make it convenient for your ma. You know. 'Cause a lotta times when she stop over my house, she on her way to work. And I don't want her to have to pull the skin back. I want her to get in, suck it, and get out.

Women like people to talk and shit when you make love and having sex, whatever you wanna call it. Women are always at me, "Why don't you say something? Talk to me. Is it good to you? I don't know—say something." You're on my shit, you know. Who gonna win the championship? I don't know. Have you ever been fuckin' so good—the girl turn around and give you a look like she—you're hitting doggy style, right, and she turn around and give you this confused look on her face. But it's good to her but she just got that look like she's confused. She turn around like this. "Hey." And you don't know what to say, once again. "Oh, shit, you all right? Everything cool? Okay, well, keep your eyes on the road, I'm driving back here. I got that." You know, motherfucker likes to talk and all that stuff. Richard Pryor once said, "If your lady don't go to sleep after you did some fuckin', then you got some more fuckin' to do." Oh, yeah. Well, I guess I always have some fuckin' to do. I can't pay a motherfucker to go to sleep. 'Cause women can chit-chat after you fuck, can't they? "And so anyway, I was tellin' Chemise about the—" And you're tryin' not to fall asleep on their ass. You're like, "All right. Right. Right. Right." You ain't even talking on the same subject they're on. "Right. Right. I love Oreo cookies, you know." "I ain't said shit about no goddamned Oreo cookies. Wake your ass up." "I'm sorry, what was you saying, baby, what was you saying?"

YOU SO CRAZY

81

See when you finished, man, I know a lotta brothers, we wonder, after women, 'cause we wanna know if you're happy, if you came. We wanna know. But don't ask 'em, man. Don't ask a woman if she came. Just go the fuck to sleep. And then in the morning, she'll tell you, "You know what? You know, I didn't come last night?" "What? You didn't come? Why didn't you say something? No, I'd'a took care of you. I'd'a hugged you up. Well, shit, I'll be back from work in a couple of hours. I'll do you right then."

But if you ask her right afterwards, "Did you come?" "No, I didn't." Now you gotta like this. "All right. Hold up. All right. Let me get my shit back up. Come on. Come on. Baby, lick me right here. Lick me right here. That's where—" And you know when the woman wants more. 'Cause she don't want you to take the dick out. She's like, "No, no, don't move—lay here. Lay here. Don't move." And you're like, "You feel the motherfucker going down? It's slipping out anyway."

I love to get my dick sucked. That ain't no secret. I likes me a little head. I like to watch too. I didn't like to watch. I used to didn't wanna look, cause I didn't wanna embarrass the girl and shit. I used to peek and, you know, look at her, peek. But now I look. I say, "Look here, baby, I'm gonna look. I'm gonna see what's makin' me feel so good." Some women don't give a fuck. "Well, I don't give a fuck, motherfucker." "You live around here?" Sisters like to examine the dick before they give you head, man. The ones I came in contact with. "Uh-huh, hold on. Wait a minute. Uh-huh. I don't just go down, be suckin' nobody's dick. Huh-huh. That ain't me. I don't just go down. Suckin' nobody's dick. You know, turn on the light. Turn on the light. What's this? What's the blue thing? What's the blue thing?" Brothers tryin' to play it on. "Go ahead, girl, that's a mole. Go ahead, now. Handle that." White girls don't give a fuck. "It looks like blueberries."

'Cause I do believe in that, man, if you do me, I do you back. Not all the time. No, I'm saying I gotta get to know you. 'Cause I didn't use to do that. My lady, "Baby, do your baby." "No. You can't cook, I don't eat it. Don't ask me no more." But I started doing it and I kinda like it. Now I'm addicted to the shit. Man, I go up to women I don't even know, "Hi, how you doing?"

But it's wild though, man, 'cause I found out as much as I would like to do each and every single woman here tonight, you can't do everybody, man. No, 'cause some of you don't wash your ass. You know who you are. You're sitting out there right now, pussy smell like bacon bits, right now. The shit humming. That shit ain't right. You know who you are. 'Cause sometimes, ladies, you take them panties off and you smell the shit, act like you don't know it. Pussy smells so bad it causes havoc in the house. The dog done bit the cat. Grandma hitting on the heavy bag all 'cause of that goddamned smell. More fuckin' birds outside the window looking in. I tell a woman if her pussy ain't right. "Hey, smell that girl. Shit, it smell like shit." "That's you. This—all this shit is you. That's you. Huh-huh." If you're my lady, I tell you in a minute, "Baby, douche." What is it? Dooche or douche? Well, do both of them motherfuckers. I even put that shit in for you. Give me four douches. Squash, squashy. Squash, squashy. Squash, squashy. Move, girl. Lay down, open your goddamned legs. Squash, squashy. You stop letting the water seep out. Stop letting the vinegar seep out. The vinegar needs to soak a minute. I put the vinegar water in the pussy, make you close your leg and then shake your ass. Just so it can wash around and just—I'll make you sit there for a hour. Now spit it out. Squash. That's all. Fuck it. You treat douche like mouthwash. That's all. I even tell a woman, lay your ass down here. I'll put Love My Carpet on your pussy. Now lay there and let that shit sit for five minutes. I'll come vacuum it up when I'm finished.

When you have love, you don't go through that stuff. You can talk to each other 'cause you're in love. You can say, "Baby, the pussy ain't right." She can say, "Your balls stink." 'Cause ladies done ran into some sweaty balls. Haven't you? Y'all just never been able to say anything about it. And ladies won't say nothing. They kiss some salty balls. They come up like that. I didn't ask you to season my meat.

TWELVE

You know when you're in love, man. You know when you're in love 'cause you start doing things in front of each other that you wouldn't do when you first met her. You know what I'm saying? Remember when you first met her, if you had to fart, you run outside say you got to change the tire on your car and shit. But once you get used to them, you fart in their face. Shut up. Make me another grill cheese sandwich. And women they take it, too. Won't you stop please? You're so bad. My mouth was open. You so crazy.

You ever fart in your sleep? One brother say, "How would you know, you're sleeping?" No, I mean, you fart in your sleep so loud and the shit wake you up? You think a motherfucker's knocking on the door and say, "Who the fuck there? Who's that? Who the fuck's knocking on the goddamned door?"

I did that shit one time. Very embarrassing, man, 'cause I farted and I woke up and shit and, "Oh, shit." And my lady was lying right there. And, you know, she didn't wake up so I don't know if she heard it or not. But she had this squint on her face and shit, you know. You know what I'm saying? And all day long, she's walking around like this. "What the fuck you doing all this squinting and shit for? Okay, I farted." So she didn't hear it. She just said it was her sinuses acting up, you know. Women—do you all fart? Do ladies fart? Sister's straight up. "Yes, we fart."

I ain't met a lady yet that farted in front of me. I don't think you all fart. I don't think you all poop, fart, none of that shit. I think you all know how to hold that shit real motherfuckin' good, man. That's why every time a bro' wanna make love, you go, "I can't, I can't. I got the cramps." "Well, fart, I'm ready to fart. Come on, fart." And women won't shit in front of you no matter how long they with you. When do you all shit? I think you all wait till a mo-

YOU SO CRAZY

therfucker go to sleep or work. That's why you all are always rushing us in the mornin'. "I—yeah, I'll call you. Go on. I will call you." Run in the bathroom and shit.

We walk back in the house, "You're in there shitting, ain't you, girl?" "Boy, you're so crazy. Hand me the Summer Breeze." And it's fucked up, though, man. 'Cause sometimes women could go shit at the wrong time. The wrong fuckin' time. You guys are playing around with your girl, ready to make love, "Come on, girl, my shit's ready to go, let's do this." And she go, "No, wait, I gotta use the bathroom. Wait. I'll be right back." And go take a shit. Right before you get ready to make love, she go take a shit. And then climb her shitty ass back in bed. Talking about, "I'm ready." "Oh, hell, no, you ain't." You wake up the next morning, got shit crumbs all in the goddamned bed. You're sweeping your bed like this. "Just hand me the Spic and Span, girl. Hand me the goddamned Spic and Span." But then you deal with shit when you're in love. You deal with shit when you're in love. Also when you're in love you play games, boy. Like during sex. Remember them games after you finish sex and shit. The games you play when you're in love. Baby, let's wrestle. You

know what I'm saying? Let's wrestle butt naked. I'm gonna wrestle you down. And then like I'm gonna put the dick in, okay? Is that cool. But sometimes she too goddamned strong and shit. You like . . . Wait! Hold on! Hold your motherfucker! Wait! Let's just fuck the normal way. Let's just do it the normal way.

You being working out with Lee Haney, girl? And then all the motherfuckin' games you play when you're in love. 'Cause brothers we don't give a fuck. After we get on the bed butt naked sometimes, little dick and all, just on the bed like this dancing, right . . . And she like, boy, why don't you sit your little-dick self down. You like, that's all right you know what I look like when it's grown-up.

See, I don't brag on my dick. I'll tell y'all that now. I don't brag on my dick. 'Cause I ain't—I'll tell the world, I ain't packing. Right now my shit is chilling. I know you're surprised. I ain't packing. Don't get me wrong, when I'm erect, I can hang with some of the big boys. I get in line . . . What ya'll talking about? But when I ain't erect, I'm hanging out with Webster like a motherfucker. See, I don't brag on lady how big my dick is. See, ladies know. Women know how big men's dicks are because they rub us,

they caress us. They know. When it's erect, they hold it like this. Wow. This is nice. But when they ain't erect, they hold it with two fingers. Hello? Wake up. Hello. And we never want y'all to see it or touch it. We like, turn out the light. I got a lot on my mind. My dog just died.

'Cause if you in the living room, man, makin' out and your shit is like bam, and you ready to go to work, right, said, "Girl, I'm gonna take you there, I'm gonna rock your world, I'm gonna take you there." She's like—she's like, "Well, whatever, you gonna take me there, let's come on." And you like this, "Hold up. My condom in the other room. I'll be back."

Dick stay hard, dick stay hard, dick stay hard, dick stay hard, dick stay hard, dick stay hard. Oh, shit, I stepped on a roach, my dick went down.

I figure, guys, I figure since we got to use all these condoms why did they circumsise us in the first place? Right? We could've used that extra meat, man?

Am I right or wrong? We coulda just slid that meat down, put a twistie tie on that.

THIRTEEN

Women say in the nineties we're not doing enough foreplay, guys. They say you have to do that foreplay. I don't mind doing foreplay. Just sometimes y'all ask for it at the wrong damn time. You know what I'm saying? 'Cause sometimes you just want to get in. And get out.

Like I went to see this woman, okay, I'm in Chicago, hanging out at Chig Wrigs. And I went to see a girl a hour away from where Chig Wrigs is at. Now check it out, I called her from a phone booth, I said, "Look here, girl. I'm at this club, it's four in the morning, I need to see you. I'm needing you, I'm wanting you, girl." She said "Well, it's four in the morning, is it that good to you?" I said, "It sure is, that's why I'm calling at four in the morning." She said, "Well, if it's that good then you'll get in your car and you'll drive that hour drive." I said, "You right. Bye, I'm on my way." So I jumped in my car. I said, "Shit." Driving an hour drive, four in the morning, going to get this late-night pussy. Falling asleep behind the wheel, but pussy was keeping me up. You know, I said, if I'm gonna die, you know, let me get this shit first.

So I get there and I'm ready to go to work 'cause that's a long drive. I said, "Let's do this, girl." She got mad. "Hold on, motherfucker, damn, shit, what about the foreplay?" Shit. What about the foreplay? Now that made me mad, 'cause I told her, "You could've handled that shit when I was driving over here. You want me to drive and do foreplay?" No.

I don't mind doing foreplay but, guys, you got to have nice lips. When you kiss on a woman's body your lips should just—it should be real nice, it should be like mmmwa, mmwa, mmwa, mmwa. You shouldn't have them hard-ass, crusty, fucked-up lips. . . .

Kissing on her body. Talkin' about mmwa, mmwa, mmwa, mmwa, mmwa. "Ouch, motherfucker, you cut me."

YOU SO CRAZY

Well, pour some water on your damn lips. I love the way women give foreplay. Y'all are the best, I got to give you your propers, y'all the best. You get like a little kid. But I hate that amateur. Don't know what the fuck she's doing. Thinks she's too pretty. You know who I'm talking about, pecking and shit. Get ahead and kiss it right on the motherfucker.

Some women you don't have to do much though, foreplay, you don't. You could just blow on their hair and they get hot. They just—oohh, ooohh, waow. You know. But some women you got to go to work. You be kissing, talking about, mmwa, mmwa, mmwa. That ain't going to get it, motherfucker. 'Cause you know what they want.

I like doing that shit. I didn't know it was so good, man. I'm mad I just started yesterday.

I did. I didn't know it was so good. Oh, man, yeah, it was good, man, but you can't do everybody. I'm serious, you can't. 'Cause some of them motherfuckers are a little tart.

You be down there. Some of 'em taste like they put seasoning salt on and shit. Say, I didn't order no fuckin' steak. Women go, go wash yours, yeah, fuck you.

I'm telling you I recommend it. If you're not

doing it, you have to do it. You know why? Because you can't beat the response. 'Cause if you do it right, women, you go, women go off, they be, oh, my, oh, you, that's to make you go. . . . And if you do it that good, they grab your head and they look at you. And they ask you, "What is your name?"

FOURTEEN

Now, that's my sport, boxing. A lotta people don't know that. That's my motherfuckin' sport. I used to box. And I was good, yeah, I was a motherfucker here, like ba-bam. And I used to move all the time 'cause I didn't wanna get hit, you know. I thought I was gonna grow up and look finer than a motherfucker so I didn't want nobody busting that up. But I used to move, boy, all the time, like jazz. I was like Ali with my shit. You know, just dancing, moving. My coach had a good saying about me, "One thing about Martin, he ain't gonna get hit. And he ain't gonna hit nobody." 'Cause I dance all motherfuckin' night. Ding.

"Good round, motherfucker, good round."

YOU SO CRAZY

'Cause my thing was, I didn't wanna get knocked out, man. That's too motherfuckin' embarrassing. Pow, to get knocked and shit. You know, you brothers get knocked, bam, don't even know where they at. Now, bam, "Give me a Caesar salad, a bag o' Twizzlers, all that shit, man. Two bus passes." Motherfuckers don't know where they are and need two bus passes, man. You know, and what do you say to the motherfucker if he's a friend that got knocked out? You driving home with this motherfucker and you like, "Shew, damn. Did he hit you as hard as it fuckin' looked, man? No, I ain't found your teeth. I don't know where them motherfuckers are at."

See, that's why I thought like if you're a fighter, you should be humbler than a motherfucker, man. When you walk to the ring, shut the fuck up, don't say nothing when you go in the fight. Just walk in the ring and fight. And if you get knocked out, you know, you're tell the media, "Fuck y'all. I ain't telling you motherfuckers I wasn't gonna get knocked out. I ain't said shit."

See, you got brothers that walk in and talk a good game and get knocked out, then they're embarrassed afterward. 'Cause before the fight, they—you can ask 'em, "What is your strategy for the fight?" And those motherfuckers, "Well, as you well know, I have the best jab in the business. Uh, I feel better than I've ever felt in my life. I'm in the best condition of my life. What I plan on doing is coming out the first couple of rounds, throwing the jab which is the best jab in the business, I'm gonna hit him a couple of times, soften up the face. I'm probably going to the body on him. See, I'm a people's choice. People like me. I'm the champ, you understand? I can't see the fight going any other way. I'm gonna hurt the boy. I'm gonna hurt him bad. I can't see it going any other way."

Then the nigger get in the ring, it's some different shit, right. Bam. Motherfucker's different shit. His speech is like this. "What happened?" "Uh, okay, well, I came out and I tried to use the jab that I had told you that was supposed to be the best jab in the business, I put it out there, he came over with a right hand. I went to my right leg but see, I had hurt that in practice. I was abused as a child and a lotta people don't know this shit." Fuck that shit; don't say nothing, man.

And boxers kill me 'cause everybody has a motherfuckin' shout-out. You know, when they win or whatever. They wanna get in front of the camera and say hello to everybody. Black people especially.

We got shout-outs for your ass. "Just won the belt this year. Ray. Irv. Cha-cha. A-a-a—all the motherfuckers that down at se'en-eleven, you know, bringing the belt home. Yeah, well, I told you boys."

White people don't do all that shit, man. They get right to the fuckin' point: "Tucson, Arizona, coming home." They don't do all that shit, man. Y'all want a white heavyweight champion bad, don't ya? That's all right, say it, sir. It's all right. You want a white, heavyweight champion, don't ya? Say it, goddamnit, say what you—There you go, man. See, it's coming out, isn't it? "Goddammit, Martin, I want one." That's what I wanna hear you say, man. This is America. You can say what you want. It's all right to feel you wanna white heavyweight champion. Shit ain't gonna happen. Shit just ain't gonna motherfucker happen. Long as a brother outta work, this shit just not gonna happen. You got some brother that will beat your ass for two dollars and a biscuit, motherfucker.

Boxin' is rough. You know what I'm saying? 'Cause see women love fighters; ladies feel protected by fighters. You motherfuckers felt like, oh, if somebody hits you, pow, "Baby, hit the motherfucker, hey, man." You know a fighter: "Don't you ever put your motherfucker hand on my lady." If Mike Tyson smacked my lady, shit, I'd fight Mike Tyson. For smacking my lady. Let's think about this shit now, you all. You know, 'cause this is Mike Tyson. You know what I'm saying? I know, I wanna jump on him, but I got to think before I go jumping on Mike. I gotta think, How good has my girl been to me? And is this bitch worth dying for? Fuck all that.

I try to get outta fight quicker than a motherfuck. Mike Tyson can smack my lady right in front of me, pow. I'm like, "Hey, hey, man, Mike, Mike, hold on, man. Hold on. What happened? What'd she do? What's the problem? Uh-huh. Well, she does that shit a lot. She does that a lot. Well, look, go on about your business, man, you're in enough trouble. Stop that shit, man. Girl, get the fuck outta here and leave Mike alone. You know he's got some shit on his mind."

I ain't fighting no Mike, man, for nobody. Well, if Mike hit my mother, I guess I have to fight, huh? I don't know though, man. 'Cause I—you know, man, that's Mike Tyson, I got to think. I know that's my mom but I got to think first. You know? How good has my mom been to me coming up? I never did get them Nikes I wanted, you know. . . .

FIFTEEN

I'm working out. 'Cause I did a movie with Eddie Murphy, *Boomerang*. And I was very fat. Eddie wanted me to look fat 'cause he didn't want me looking better than him. He know I have potential for the ladies. So he didn't want me to look better. But that was cool. I didn't mind. So I worked the weight off and went over to Eddie's house during the movie. Wow. Eddie has a beautiful fuckin' house, man. I walked in his house, this man has indoor pool, outdoor pool, bowling alley, music studio, racquet ball court. Air strip. Every goddamn thing in the house. And you walk in a big-ass house like this—it's hard to act like you ain't no bitch. See, I walked in like a bitch. Like "Ohhh. This is real nice,

Eddie, this is real nice." And I didn't wanna leave the motherfucker 'cause Eddie was like, "Well, I'm about to go to bed, you know, get some rest." And I was like, "You don't wanna bowl or nothing? Let me hear your album one more time." But you know what I found out though? Women don't leave your ass as quick when you gotta nice place, do they? Motherfucker, some of you ladies know a comfortable goddamned roof over your head when you see one.

But yeah, man, working on that weight. Get that weight down. If you're fat, you're fat, fuck it. You know what I'm saying? Fuck it, be happy. That's what's important. I love you if you're fat. I don't give a fuck. You're not fat to me. You're just bigger than a motherfucker. You are big-boned. That's all you are to me. I love you. Women always worrying about their weight. They worry about their stomachs and shit. Little pouches and shit. Fuck that. I likes a little pouch. I likes me a little pouch every now and then. I likes to hit it from the side and pat that pouch.

Motherfucker's always worrying about the pouch. Stop it. You know, I don't like women that got racks and shit. You start storing socks and shit in the motherfucker. Look, baby, put the dope under your tittie. Put it under your tittie. Well, then, put it in the

back then. No, right down there. Tape the shit down. Be playing her side and shit like that. No. I'm just saying, stop worrying about your weight. And what kills me, when people make excuses for being fat. There ain't no excuse. "It's my metabolism." No, it is not. It's some Twizzlers in your back goddamned pocket. Let the Reese's cups go. Get outta the Häagen Dazs line. And it's fucked up when you see 'em in the line and they look at you and you — you know, in a line when they're getting ready to buy ice cream and shit. 'Cause they look at you and like, "Yeah, and?"

People tell you that they love you when you're fat, but they don't tell you the truth. I'm gonna tell you the truth 'cause that's the kinda motherfucker I am. That's who I am. If you're weighin' over 250, stay the fuck outta Spandex. Okay? Stay the fuck outta Spandex. That shit don't look good. Like a bag o' knots in your ass. Like a gang of fists chilling in your ass. And fat women kill me always working out in leotards and shit with tights on and shit—working out in tights and all that shit. No, no, sweatsuits. Glad bags. Sweat it out. Let the shit out. You know, always worrying about your weight. Stop it. Lose it. Lose the worrying about his weight.

YOU SO CRAZY

If you're here tonight, we love you, Luther. Man, we don't give a fuck if you skinny or fat. We love you, Luther. Luther always losing weight. We love Luther. Always losing the weight. We don't give a fuck if you're fat. I just want you to do the slow songs. Stick to the slow songs, and stop doing all the fast songs. Talking about having a party. You don't—your big ass gonna faint. Stop it, Luther.

And then Luther come on stage with all that goddamned glitter on. Talking about, "How y'all feel?" You gonna faint with all that goddamned glitter on. Like a big-ass glitter ball. Oprah, too. I love Oprah. But, Oprah, you gotta stop it. Make up your mind. You gonna be skinny or fat? Make up your goddamned mind. We don't give a fuck if Oprah fat.

Remember when Oprah had the show where she lost all the goddamned weight? Came out, brung all the meat in a bag; ground beef and everything in a goddamned bag. "This is what I lost. This is what I lost." Well, apparently when she left, she ate the motherfucker. 'Cause damn if she didn't come back the next day looking like the old big-ass Oprah, "Color Purple" Oprah.

And I didn't like the way Michael Jackson treated Oprah. I love Michael but I didn't like the way Michael did Oprah. When she come into his house, he prepared for Oprah. Michael, that's a sister coming to see you and talk to you; you didn't have to prepare for Oprah, Michael. You notice, 'cause he didn't know who was coming to see him, you know—the little Oprah or the big Oprah. He wasn't gonna have Oprah fuckin' his shit up. Mike paid too much money for his shit. You notice when she was interviewing Michael was in a chair, Oprah was on a bench. Like tell me about your life. What happened? And remember that—remember the alarm went off? Pow, pow, pow, pow. And Oprah was like, "We'll be right back. Somebody's trying to get in Mike's door. We're gonna check that out. We'll be back." Shit. There weren't nobody trying to get in Mike's door. That was the goddamned bench alarm going, "Yah, yah, yah, yah. This motherfucker too big, man."

I got to talk about Michael too, fuck it. You know, ain't nothing changed. Shit. I love Michael. Got to meet him. Michael, the baddest entertainer in the world. How many motherfuckers could say, "You know, I'm jamming in Bucharest next week, right?" You's a bad motherfucker when you got them motherfuckers jumping. 'Cause all they wanna do is blow up shit. "If you ain't good, we're blowing it up.

Go on, motherfucker." No, I think Michael's mad, man. I think he's pimping broads. I think once them cameras off, Michael's like this, "Look-look, look, bitch, don't-don't play with me. Make me a motherfuckin' sandwich. Beat it. Make me a goddamned sandwich. Let's fuck around, Brooke. Got a little of my father in me, now don't fuck around, now."

Remember on the interview with Liz Taylor? "I wanna say a few words about Michael." And Michael was in the back looking at Liz like this, rocking. Remember when he was rocking, he was listening his ass off like, "Bitch, don't you tell Oprah no shit I don't want her to know. You shouldn't been out this motherfucker, girl."

And you know what fucked me up? Michael wanted to meet me though. That fucked me up. Michael Jackson, man, wanted to meet me. I said, "Damn." And it was a trip 'cause his security came and got me. This kid acting like it was some big CIA shit. You know, walk up to me and, "Uh, excuse me, Martin. Yeah, well, look here. Uhhh, Michael will meet you." "Michael who, motherfucker? Michael from *Good Times*? Michael who?" Motherfucker's talking about Michaelll. I said, "Michael who, motherfucker?" He said, "Michaelllll." And I was like, "Oh, shit. Michael wanna meet me?"

Now I thought when I meet Michael Jackson I would walk in there and just stay myself. Be myself. You know, just walk in, "Yo, what's up, Mike? Pleasure to meet you, you know, just doing my thing. You know. Fuckin' with the white people. Oops. No offense, Mike." Didn't even go down. But it was different 'cause I walked in and I felt like a little bitch. And once again the shit just came out. I went in doing medleys and shit of Michael's songs.

But what fucked me up was Michael shook my hand and he jumped back. Motherfucker said, "Oh, ahhhh. Ohhhh." "What the fuck you jumping for, man? You asked to meet me, Michael, I didn't ask to meet you." And Ms. Jackson was sitting in the corner and I hadn't seen her. I say, "Hey, how you doing, Miz. Jackson?" And she jumped up, "Joe, stop beating the kids. Joe, stop beating the kids." And I had to calm her down. "No, Miz. Jackson, no. I was explaining to Michael, I loved it in 'Beat It.' No, I didn't—he didn't say nothin' about beating the kids. Everything—I'm Martin. Yeah, 'Beat It,' the music, his song. No, I'm not the one who hit LaToya with the chair, Mz. Jackson. Calm down. I did not hit LaToya. Well, you said the bitch was psychic. She shoulda known the chair was coming."

That whole Michael Jackson thing, man, I believe Joe. I guess that's the kinda motherfucker I am. I think Joe didn't do nothing. He beat them kids like you're supposed to beat kids. You know what I'm saying? That's all Joe did. Just whoop a little ass. I saw Joe on Geraldo. You know Geraldo; he'll get the motherfuckin' story one way or another. He can get hit by a truck for the story. That motherfucker gets stabbed in the eye by the Klansmen. Be like this. "Well, as you know, I'm outside the Klansman home. They just stabbed me in the eye. We'll be back on the next edition of Geraldo."

Well, Geraldo got on Joe's shit, you know, and was like, "Did you beat the kids?" Joe beat their ass like normal black fathers whip a ass. Joe went off. "I'm tired of this shit. This is bullshit, Ilaldo. I didn't beat them goddamned kids. Okay, I hit Michael one goddamned time. I told him to save Tito some syrup. That's all that shit was about. I'm tired of everybody fuckin' with me, Ilaldo."

See, white people, y'all too sensitive about ass-whuppin'. I gotta explain that to the white people that are here tonight. That's how we whip a ass. Black people—it's like a lion with the cub. It look like you're hurting 'em but you're not. Black people whup ass, "Like get your ass up out the thing. Get your ass up out the goddamned thing. Get your ass off the thing. Get your ass off the—bitch, come on, get your ass off." That's how black people whup ass.

White people—y'all way too sensitive with your goddamned kids. You can save yourself all that goddamned stress. 'Cause when your child start acting up, get in his ass right then and there. 'Cause you all let your kid fuck up. Motherfucker could be standing on top of a monument, white people stand there all day, "Eric, get down. Eric, get down. Eric. Eric, get down. I'm gonna leave you. I'm leaving, Eric."

Black people ain't going through that shit. Black kids ain't embarrassing the black parents. We ain't gonna b, out there like that, "Get down. Get down. I ain't gonna tell you no more, get down." Huh-huh. Black people hire a motherfucker sniper. "Uh-huh, come here. Uh-huh. Motherfucker, that's my child. Do what the fuck I say. Okay. Do what the fuck I say. Shoot him in his ass right now. No, I don't want you to kill him. I want his ass to fall hard." Next time that motherfucker come to a mall, he be limping. Motherfucker go into Foot Locker, "Give me one shoe. One shoe, motherfucker."

SIXTEEN

Anybody here smoke herb? When I say herb, I gotta explain that to the white people. Reefer, you know. Black people and white people get high differently. I mean, you hit the joint but it affects us differently. You see a brother hit a joint, "Yeah, motherfucker. Yeah, this is some good shit. That's some good shit there. That's a good shit there. Oh, shit, that's some good shit there, nigger." Brothers hit a joint and just cool out. Mellow out. Just—"Yeah, ahhh. Go ahead, nigger. Ahhh, who is saying that? Ohhh."

White people? You motherfuckers hit a joint and start on some other shit. "Wow. Did you hear that, man? Says 'Kill four people.' Just kill four people." That shit affect people differently and shit. And every motherfucker that gets high makes an excuse for why they get high, man. Hit a joint, talking about, "You know they say this cure cancer, right?" Like if you got the gout in your motherfuckin' leg, this shit knock that shit right the fuck out. You don't even feel the gout, man. "Hit that shit, man." And them motherfuckers hit it, "Damn, you right, 'cause I had some tension right here, man, that shit feel good."

But brothers analyze everything when they're smoking that herb, man. You analyze every motherfuckin' thing. I broke up in a relationship over that shit; I hit a joint, right, and I looked at my girl. I say, "Erica?" "Yes, it's Erica, motherfucker, who the fuck you think it is, motherfucker?" "Your motherfuckin' left eye is damn near on the side of your motherfuckin' head. Your eyes are spread the fuck apart. What the fuck is wrong?" I said, "We got to end this shit. We got to end this shit, 'cause now we no longer see eye to eye. You know what I'm saying? We ain't gonna be fuckin' and you looking at everybody in the other room. I ain't gonna have that shit. Uh-huh."

And don't get high and drive across country with your boy. I mean, just be careful who you take the goddamned trips with, you never know. Especially a long motherfuckin' trip. You know what I mean. I took a trip and found out like, you know, it was cool, see that was his thing; found out my boy was gay, you know. No, I did. It took a trip—we took a cross-country trip, I found out he was gay, you know, uh, you know, I don't like to call him faggot but, you know, I found out, you know, the boy was gay. And it fucked me up 'cause he just jumped out the closet on the motherfucker. You know what I'm saying? I don't mind—if you're a friend of mine, I don't mind you coming out the closet, but ease out that motherfucker, man. Ease. Just tip out the motherfucker. Look before you crash open the door, man. Take your time. "This is who I am."

I had a motherfucker do that to me, man. Came out the closet, "Hi." You know. 'Cause we was driving across country and the shit fucked me up 'cause I knew he was overnice to me. I was driving and I was a little tense, so I started cracking my neck, and so he looked up and he saw me doing this shit. He said, "Damn, you look a little tense, you wanna brother to lean over and crack your back? Crack your neck? Loosen you the fuck up? You know, help your driving."

I looked at him. "Motherfucker, I don't need you to lean over and crack my goddamned neck, man. Loosen me the fuck up. I ain't no faggot, no punk. I ain't all of that, man, I ain't with that shit." And he got mad. "Man, you ain't gonna be no punk, no faggot, no nothing, no like that, gay or some shit like that, man, to let a brother crack your neck, your back, loosen you up. I'm trying to help your motherfuckin' driving." I was like, "Damn, motherfucker, you're right. You're right. You know, because I'm jumping to conclusions. What harm can it do, you know?"

And sure enough, he leaned over, crack, crack, crack, and I was like "Damn, motherfucker. Damn, the nigger's kind. Yeah." You know, I was like in there.

So then we got in the city like when it was real hot. And I was like "Phew." And he woke up. And he was, you know, "I noticed you phew." And I said, "Yeah, well, you know, I'm a little hot." He said, "Well, you want me to go in my cup, you know, and get some ice outta my cup and put it on your neck and let the water drip down and cool your body off, or something like that?"

"What the fuck you talking about, man? I ain't

gay, no punk. I ain't with that shit. I ain't no faggot, no punk. I don't need you going in your cup getting no ice, putting it on my neck, letting the water drip down, cooling me the fuck off, man." He got mad. "Man, you ain't gotta be no punk, no faggot, no gay, or some shit like that. You know what I'm saying? And let somebody go in their cup, put ice on your neck and let the water drip down and cool you off." You know, and I was like, "You're right. You're right. I keep jumping to co-fuckin' conclusions. Why am I getting upset? Please, do you have any ice?" Sure enough, he got the ice. "Whoa. Thank you." So he was so nice to me.

'Bout the time we got to Cleveland, I asked him to suck my dick. He was a little hesitant about that though, like, "No, I don't know. I don't know." I was like, "Come on, man, you ain't gotta be no faggot or no-no punk to do that shit, man. A nigger is tense right now. I'm trying to get to Maryland, mother-fucker."